August/Agosto

By/Por Robyn Brode

Reading Consultant/Consultora de lectura: Linda Cornwell,
Literacy Connections Consulting/consultora de lectoescritura

WEEKLY READER®
PUBLISHING

Please visit our web site at **www.garethstevens.com**.
For a free catalog describing our list of high-quality books, call 1-800-542-2595 (USA) or 1-800-387-3178 (Canada). Our fax: 1-877-542-2596

Library of Congress Cataloging-in-Publication Data
Brode, Robyn.
   [August. Spanish & English]
   August / by Robyn Brode ; reading consultant, Linda Cornwell = Agosto / por Robyn Brode ; consultora de lectura, Linda Cornwell.
      p. cm. — (Months of the year = Meses del año)
   English and Spanish in parallel text.
   Includes bibliographical references and index.
   ISBN-10: 1-4339-1936-2   ISBN-13: 978-1-4339-1936-7 (lib. bdg.)
   ISBN-10: 1-4339-2113-8   ISBN-13: 978-1-4339-2113-1 (softcover)
   1. August (Month)—Juvenile literature. 2. Vacations—United States—Juvenile literature.
I. Cornwell, Linda. II. Title. III. Title: Agosto.
GT4803.B76313   2010
394.263—dc22   2009014212

This edition first published in 2010 by
Weekly Reader® Books
An Imprint of Gareth Stevens Publishing
1 Reader's Digest Road
Pleasantville, NY 10570-7000 USA

Executive Managing Editor: Lisa M. Herrington
Senior Editors: Barbara Bakowski, Jennifer Magid-Schiller
Designer: Jennifer Ryder-Talbot
Translators: Tatiana Acosta and Guillermo Gutiérrez

Photo Credits: Cover, back cover, title, pp. 7, 11, 19, 21 © Ariel Skelley/Weekly Reader; p. 9 © Stockbyte/Getty Images; p. 13 © Monkey Business Images/Shutterstock; p. 15 © Hill Street Studios/Getty Images; p. 17 © Comstock/Corbis

Printed in the United States of America

1 2 3 4 5 6 7 8 9 10 11 10 09

Table of Contents/Contenido

Boldface words appear in the glossary.
- - - - - - - - -
Las palabras en **negrita** aparecen en el glosario.

Welcome to August!

August is the eighth month of the year. It has 31 days. August is a **summer** month.

- - - - - - - - -

¡Bienvenidos a agosto!

Agosto es el octavo mes del año. Tiene 31 días. Agosto es uno de los meses del **verano**.

Months of the Year/Meses del año

Month/Mes	Number of Days/ Días en el mes
1 January/Enero	31
2 February/Febrero	28 or 29*/28 ó 29*
3 March/Marzo	31
4 April/Abril	30
5 May/Mayo	31
6 June/Junio	30
7 July/Julio	31
8 August/Agosto	**31**
9 September/Septiembre	30
10 October/Octubre	31
11 November/Noviembre	30
12 December/Diciembre	31

*February has an extra day every fourth year./Febrero tiene un día extra cada cuatro años.

Summer Weather

In some places, August is the hottest month. Many kids like to cool off in a **pool**. Always have a grown-up watch you when you are in a pool.

- - - - - - - - - -

Tiempo de verano

En algunos lugares, agosto es el mes más caluroso del año. A muchos niños les gusta refrescarse en una **piscina**. Cuando estés en una piscina, siempre debe haber un adulto vigilando.

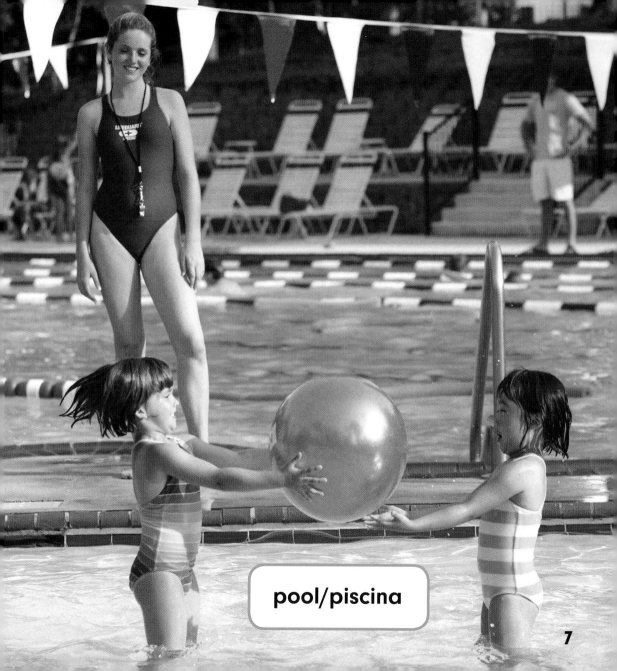

pool/piscina

Another favorite place to cool off is the beach. People enjoy splashing in the ocean.

— — — — — — — — —

La playa es otro buen lugar para refrescarse. A la gente le gusta chapotear en el océano.

What do you like to do in summer?

— — — — — — —

¿Qué te gusta hacer en el verano?

Being outside in the warm air is fun. Be careful not to get sunburned. Use **sunscreen** and wear a hat.

— — — — — — — — — —

Cuando hace calor, es divertido estar al aire libre. Ten cuidado de no quemarte con el sol. Échate **protector solar** y ponte un sombrero.

sunscreen/
protector solar

In warm, sunny August, berries are ready for picking. Mmmm! They taste good.

– – – – – – – – – –

Con el calor y el sol de agosto, las bayas están en su punto. ¡Mmmmm! Son deliciosas.

 What is your favorite summer fruit?
– – – – – – – –
¿Cuál es tu fruta de verano favorita?

strawberries/
fresas

13

Vacation Time

In August, many families go on summer **vacation**. Some families take their pets with them!

- - - - - - - - - -

Época de vacaciones

En agosto, muchas familias se van de **vacaciones** de verano. ¡Algunas se llevan a sus mascotas!

14

Many people go camping during summer vacation. They may sleep outdoors in a **tent**.

— — — — — — — — —

En las vacaciones de verano, muchas personas se van de acampada. Pueden dormir al aire libre dentro de una **tienda de campaña**.

tent/tienda de campaña

In August, some kids go back to school. They meet new **classmates**.

— — — — — — — — — —

En agosto, algunos niños vuelven a la escuela. Allí conocen a sus nuevos **compañeros de clase**.

classmates/
compañeros de clase

19

When August ends, it is time for September to begin. Soon it will be fall.

— — — — — — — — — —

Cuando agosto termina, empieza septiembre. Pronto llegará el otoño.

Glossary/Glosario

classmates: members of the same class at school

pool: a tank of water built for swimming

summer: the season between spring and fall, when the weather is the warmest of the year

sunscreen: a lotion used to prevent sunburn

tent: a shelter of fabric stretched over poles

vacation: time away from school or work

— — — — — — — — — —

compañeros de clase: miembros de una misma clase en la escuela

piscina: estanque de agua que se usa para nadar

protector solar: crema que evita las quemaduras al tomar el sol

tienda de campaña: estructura de tela, sostenida por palos, donde podemos guarecernos

vacaciones: periodo de descanso de las actividades de la escuela o del trabajo

verano: la estación del año entre la primavera y el otoño. Es la época más calurosa del año.

For More Information/Más información

Books/Libros

Beaches/Playas. Water Habitats/Hábitats acuáticos (series). JoAnn Early Macken (Gareth Stevens Publishing, 2006)

Summer/Verano. Seasons of the Year/Las estaciones del año (series). JoAnn Early Macken (Gareth Stevens Publishing, 2006)

Web Sites/Páginas web

Kids' Turn Central: Summer Fun/Diversión veraniega
www.kidsturncentral.com/summer/summerfun.htm
Find a list of fun summer activities./Encuentren una lista de divertidas actividades veraniegas.

Splash Zone USA/*Splash Zone* Estados Unidos
www.splashzoneusa.com/home.html
Play games, do puzzles, and learn about water safety./ Encuentren juegos y rompecabezas y aprendan normas de seguridad en el agua.

Publisher's note to educators and parents: Our editors have carefully reviewed these web sites to ensure that they are suitable for children. Many web sites change frequently, however, and we cannot guarantee that a site's future contents will continue to meet our high standards of quality and educational value. Be advised that children should be closely supervised whenever they access the Internet.

Nota de la editorial a los padres y educadores: Nuestros editores han revisado con cuidado las páginas web para asegurarse de que son apropiadas para niños. Sin embargo, muchas páginas web cambian con frecuencia, y no podemos garantizar que sus contenidos futuros sigan conservando nuestros elevados estándares de calidad y de interés educativo. Tengan en cuenta que los niños deben ser supervisados atentamente siempre que accedan a Internet.

Index/Índice

About the Author

Robyn Brode has been a teacher, a writer, and an editor in the book publishing field for many years. She earned a bachelor's degree in English literature from the University of California, Berkeley.

Información sobre la autora

Robyn Brode ha sido maestra, escritora y editora de libros durante muchos años. Obtuvo su licenciatura en literatura inglesa en la Universidad de California, Berkeley.